SHARKS
THE PERFECT PREDATORS

Writer and Photographer, *Howard Hall*
Series Editor, *Vicki León* **Design,** *Ashala Nicols Lawler*

SILVER BURDETT PRESS

© 1995 Silver Burdett Press
Published by Silver Burdett Press.
A Simon & Schuster Company
299 Jefferson Road,
Parsippany, NJ 07054
Printed in the United States of America
10 9 8 7 6 5 4 3 2 1

CLOSE-UP
A Focus on Nature

SILVER BURDETT PRESS
© 1995 Silver Burdett Press
Published by Silver Burdett Press.
A Simon & Schuster Company
299 Jefferson Road, Parsippany, NJ 07054
Printed in the United States of America
10 9 8 7 6 5 4 3 2 1

Library of Congress
Cataloging-in-Publication Data
Hall, Howard, 1949-
Sharks: the perfect predators/ by Howard Hall;
photographs by Howard Hall.
p.cm.-- (Close up)
ISBN 0-382-24891-0 (LSB)
ISBN 0-382-24892-9 (SC)
1. Sharks–Juvenile literature.
[1. Sharks.] I. Title. II. Series: Close up
(Parsippany, N.J.)
QL638.9. H35 1994
597'.31–dc20
94-31828
CIP
AC

When sharks appear, human fear follows. Does our visceral reaction to this beautiful predator make sense? Marine photographer and author Howard Hall says no. "Most sharks won't harm us. Sharks, however, have good reason to fear humans."

Join Howard as we plunge into the oceans of the world to meet species such as the blue shark and its silvery admirers pictured on these pages. In the process, you'll learn the vital role sharks play in the checks and balances of the seas, and why their populations are declining.

400 MILLION YEARS
OF
SHARKS

ONE HUNDRED FEET BENEATH the surface of the Sea of Cortez, I knelt next to a large boulder and looked up to see a school of 400 hammerhead sharks. The sky darkened as they began to pass overhead. Soon the school extended to the horizon in all directions, their silhouettes passing like squadrons of bombers against the twilight.

I held my breath, eliminating the flow of bubbles from my SCUBA equipment. I was afraid that the sharks would see me, but not for the reason you might expect. Like most sharks, hammerheads feed on fish and squid. They were no more likely to attack and eat me than I was likely to attack and eat a pine tree growing in my front yard.

But I knew that if the sharks saw me or heard the sound produced by my exhaust bubbles, they would scatter like a flock of flushed quail. So I held my breath as long as I could and watched as hundreds of hammerheads crowded the waters between me and the surface. Their strange wing-shaped heads and swept-back pectoral fins made them look more like futuristic spacecraft than living creatures.

Finally I could hold my breath no longer. As I exhaled, the air rushed skyward, giving my presence away. The sharks bolted. Hundreds of powerful tail fins churned the water, producing a sound like distant thunder. In the space of a heartbeat, the entire school vanished.

HAMMERHEADS ARE AMONG THE *oddest-looking creatures on earth. Why did this shark move its eyes to either end of a head shaped like a vacuum cleaner attachment? Why do they sometimes school in great numbers? These are just two of the things we have yet to learn.*

Many times I've had the luck to see hammerhead schools. These brief glimpses always fill me with exhilaration and awe. Each time I hope to glean more insight into how they live. Why do they form schools? For what purpose did their bizarre axe-shaped heads evolve? Where do they go to mate and to have their young? Researchers don't know the answers to these questions yet. In fact, the most amazing thing about sharks may be how little we know about them! Two decades ago, scientists had identified 250 species of sharks in the world's oceans. Today we know there are more than 350 species. Fourteen of these species are known from only one specimen. Only one of each of these has ever been seen! Without a doubt there are even more species yet to be discovered.

Most people think of sharks as terrifying creatures. Many imagine that the monster made famous by author Peter Benchley and the makers of the film *Jaws* is a typical shark. Not so. *Jaws* was a fantasy. Real sharks are no more like *Jaws* than your pet dog is like *Cujo*. Ironically, the popularity of this horror fantasy has spawned a generation of diving research biologists who are fascinated with sharks and dedicated to uncovering the truth about these much-maligned animals. Their discoveries continue to reveal a fascinating and highly evolved creature of great complexity and sophistication.

Sharks have been called primitive creatures. Although accurate in some ways, this description is misleading. Sharks first began to appear on earth about 400 million years ago. They roamed the seas 200 million years before dinosaurs walked on land, and beat humans on the scene by some 399 million years. This does not mean their biological design is antiquated – just the opposite. Sharks have survived on this planet so long (some species virtually unchanged for nearly 100 million years) because the process of evolution has refined them to near-perfection.

Over the millenia, many species of sharks have passed into extinction. The 350 species alive today

SHARKS HAVE SEVERAL COUSINS WITH SKELETONS MADE OF CARTILAGE ALSO: RAYS, SUCH AS THE MANTA BEING "DRIVEN" AT TOP LEFT; SKATES; AND THE ODD CHIMAERA OR RATFISH, PICTURED AT BOTTOM LEFT.

SHARK HABITATS
Which sharks prowl the coral reefs? The silvertip. The Galápagos. And other species such as this Caribbean reef shark.

KEEN OF EYE,
SHARKS HAVE A SHINY
TAPETUM BEHIND
THE RETINA THAT
LETS THEM SEE WELL
IN NEAR-DARKNESS.
TEETH VARY GREATLY,
AND DEPEND ON THE
SHARK'S DIET. THE
HORN SHARK AT RIGHT
USES ITS TEETH TO
GRIND CRABS, SEA
URCHINS, AND OTHER
HARD-SHELLED PREY.

represent the best in evolutionary design. Sharks are the world's most perfect predators.

As fish, sharks belong to a class of fishes called *Chondrichthyes* or cartilaginous fishes. Skates, rays, and a very odd group of fish called chimaeras also belong to this class. The most important characteristic separating cartilaginous fishes from all other fishes? Their skeleton. Sharks, rays, and chimaeras have no bones. Their muscles attach to a skeleton made entirely of cartilage. All other fishes have bony skeletons just as we do.

Chimaeras or ratfishes look bizarre, even hideous. Their long tapering bodies end in a whip-like tail. They have huge eyes for capturing what light exists at the extreme depths where they live. Their teeth are fused into plates to crush shellfish they find buried in the silt. Males have a tooth-like structure mounted on their foreheads which they probably use in some strange way during courtship and mating, although no one except a chimaera has actually seen this.

Sharks soar through the ocean like jet airplanes fly through air. Their powerful tail fins provide propulsion and their pectoral fins and the shape of their bodies provide lift. Unlike bony fishes, sharks and rays have no swim bladder to neutralize their buoyancy. If they stop swimming, they sink. Only constant forward motion keeps water flowing over the wing-like pectoral fins which hold the animal up.

Most shark tails are heterocercal, which means having larger top lobes than bottom ones. The large top lobe helps push the shark's tail down and keep its nose up. This design permits slow-swimming sharks to plane through the water in a slightly nose-up position. That also helps them keep from sinking.

The slower the cruising speed of a shark species, the larger its pectoral or chest fins tend to be. Sharks that swim at fast cruising speeds tend to have stout stubby bodies and short fins. The same kind of body design can be seen in aircraft. Glider planes fly very slowly and thus have long, narrow, sleek fuselages and extremely long wings. Jet fighters fly fast, have short fuselages and stubby wings.

A blue shark's body resembles a glider more than a fighter. Blues have narrow bodies and long pectoral fins. They spend most of their lives swimming at very slow speed in open ocean. The top lobes of their heterocercal tails gently push their heads up as they glide along on their broad, wing-like pectoral fins.

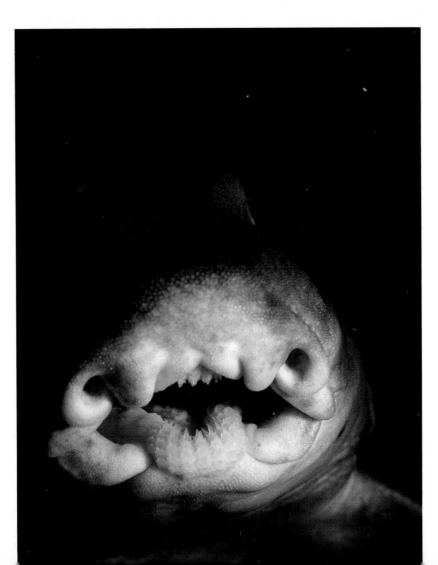

ako sharks, on the other hand, look like jet fighters. Their short, robust, almost foot-ball-shaped bodies are equipped with very short pectoral fins. Makos also have homocercal tails – the top and bottom lobes are nearly of equal size. Because the mako cruises through the ocean at high speed, it doesn't need a tail design to push its nose up.

Measuring the top swimming velocities of various sharks can be a difficult task. Most fast-swimming sharks do very poorly in captivity and wild sharks seldom cooperate for time trials in the open ocean. We do know that a shark must reach a minimum speed of 22 mph to be able to jump clear of the water. Several shark species are good jumpers; mako sharks are down-right aerobatic! Experiments with blue sharks in captivity have shown they can maintain a speed of 24.5 mph for extended periods. Some may reach 43 mph for short bursts, but not all researchers agree on this finding.

I've spent many hours underwater, watching blue sharks and mako sharks swimming in the open ocean. I can't say for certain that the blue shark can swim 43 mph. What I can say from first-hand experience is this: however fast a blue shark swims, it's practically standing still next to the speed of the mako! Mako sharks often get very aggressive toward blue sharks when they're competing with them for food. A greedy mako will sometimes chase two or three blues away, darting from one to another as the blue sharks flee at their top speed.

Do sharks ever stop swimming? It depends upon the species. Many bottom-dwelling sharks spend most of their time resting in caves and crevasses in the reef. They keep water flowing over their gills by pumping water in through the mouth and out through the gill openings. Some sharks, like the angel shark, actually spend most

Which sharks roam the open ocean? Whale sharks, biggest of the species. And filter-feeding giants like this basking shark.

of their time buried in sand waiting for an unsuspecting fish to swim overhead.

Many species never stop swimming from the moment of birth until the end of their lives. Mako sharks, white sharks, blue sharks, and others lack the musculature to pump water through their gills. They rely on constant forward motion through the water to keep oxygen-rich water passing over their gills. If they stop swimming, they stop breathing. Many sharks live more than twenty years, some perhaps as much as sixty years, and must keep swimming all the while.

It might seem that a rough, sandpaper-like skin would slow a shark down, and that a skin smooth as glass would be more hydrodynamic. But you can't beat 400 million years of evolution when it comes to good design. We've found that the sandpaper-like surface of sharkskin greatly reduces water turbulence. Sharkskin proves to be so efficient that it's been studied by the U.S. Navy for reducing drag on nuclear submarines. It's even been copied by aeronautical engineers to develop special low-drag skins for jet aircraft.

In humans and other mammals, teeth grow from jawbone. Like other bones in our bodies, our teeth should last a lifetime. But shark teeth come from the animal's skin and not from the skeleton. Special scale-like structures called denticles cover the shark's skin. Each denticle looks like a tiny shark's tooth. It is so sharp that sharkskin has served as sandpaper for many civilizations.

Shark teeth are not attached directly to the jaw but grow from a special membrane of the skin called the tooth bed. In many ways, the teeth resemble large skin denticles. Like skin denticles, the teeth constantly wear away and are replaced by new ones. In some shark species, new teeth grow to replace old ones about every ten days.

The shapes of shark teeth vary greatly, depending upon the feeding strategy of each species. Horn sharks live on the bottom, feeding

SOME SHARKS GIVE BIRTH TO LIVE BABIES. OTHERS, LIKE THE SWELL SHARK SHOWN HERE, LAY HARD EGG CASES IN WHICH THE YOUNG SHARK GROWS FOR TEN MONTHS BEFORE HATCHING ON THE SEA FLOOR.

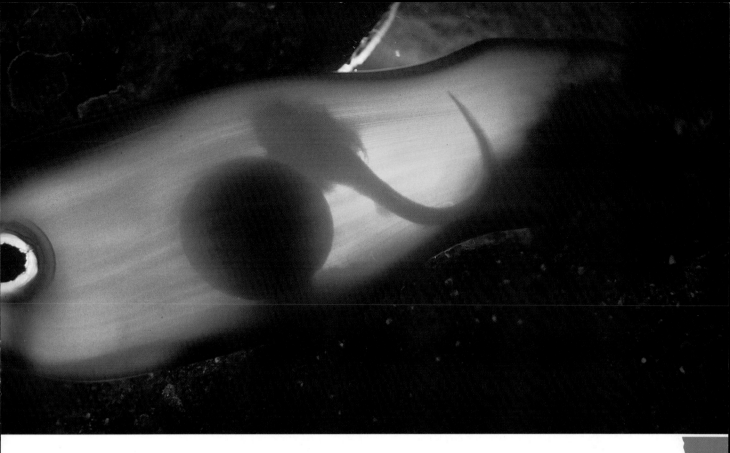

on crabs, mollusks and sea urchins. Their teeth are modified into hard plates for crushing their hard-shelled prey. The long, fang-like teeth of the mako shark are rounded in back and concave in front. The front edges rival the sharpness of the best razor blades. The jet fighters of sharks, makos pursue tuna, jacks, and mackerel at great speed, striking quickly with their teeth to inflict as much damage as possible. Makos normally swallow fish whole. Their teeth work well to snare fast-swimming fish, but are not very suitable for tearing chunks out of large prey.

The teeth of great whites, on the other hand, work fearsomely well for tearing big chunks out of prey. Their teeth are more robust and triangular than fang-like. The serrated edges of the white's teeth work like serrated knives – perfect for tearing apart large elephant seals and whales.

LIKE CERTAIN BIRDS WHICH ARE *born with a hook on their beaks for greater ease in breaking out of their shells, this baby swell shark possesses a set of hook-like scales along its back. When the time comes for it to be born, it uses them to inch forward and out.*

It's been written that an 8-foot requiem shark can produce a jaw pressure of eight tons or 16,000 pounds per square inch. While technically true, this sort of statistic is extremely misleading. You yourself can exert a similar pressure by pushing a thumbtack into a piece of wood. Your thumb may be pressing on the head of the thumbtack with a pressure of 30 pounds per square inch, but that pressure is concentrated at the sharp point of the tack and the pounds per square inch pressure of the tack point on the wood may be hundreds of times greater.

While working, I've been bitten by sharks lots of times. You would probably be surprised how difficult it can be to get a shark to bite you. Sometimes you have to work at it all day. Of course, you may say, that if it's so much trouble, why do it? In fact, you may say, why do it even if it's no trouble at all? Well, being bitten by a 10-foot-long blue shark is a very interesting sensation and can actually be rather fun. Before you do it, however, you want to make certain you dress properly. This means putting on a Neptunic anti-shark suit made of stainless steel mesh. Wearing the shark suit is fundamental to having fun when being bitten by sharks.

I can assure you that if a 10-foot-long blue shark actually did bite with a jaw pressure of eight tons, it wouldn't be any fun at all. So what does it feel like to have a shark chew on your steel mesh-protected arm? It feels as though a giant bully is squeezing your arm between his fingers and thumbs while he shakes your arm back and forth. The pressure hurts a bit and the shaking can be a little hard on your joints, but the process does no real damage.

Of course, the severity of a shark bite depends upon the size of the shark. I wouldn't want to be bitten by your average 16-foot, 3,000-pound white

SOME SHARKS SEEM MORE LIKE SKATES OR RAYS. ANGEL SHARKS, FOR INSTANCE. THEY HIDE IN SAND OR MUD, BOTH TO AMBUSH THEIR PREY AND TO KEEP FROM BEING EATEN THEMSELVES. ONE OF THEIR FAVORITE FOODS IS SQUID. AFTER SQUID MATE AND LAY EGGS, THEY DIE, THEIR BODIES PILING UP LIKE TIMBER AMONG THE EGGS. ANGEL SHARKS FIND IT EASY TO STUFF THEMSELVES AT THIS TIME.

SHARK HABITATS

*Which sharks stalk
the kelp forests?
Great whites.
Makos. And this
blue shark, looking
for squid and fish.*

ALTHOUGH THE MAINSTAY OF MOST *sharks' diet is fish, not every mouthful runs from them. Small fishes, on their own and in schools, often cruise in the proximity of a shark. Are they looking for protection or leftovers? And what does the shark get out of the deal? We don't yet know.*

BLUE SHARKS ARE JUST ONE OF *many sharks and other predators that feast on squid during their reproductive frenzy each spring. While the little cephalopods mate, spawn, and then die, the sharks gorge themselves, the black ink from a million squid bodies streaking into the water.*

shark. A shark that big could easily break arms and ribs. That would take the fun right out of it!

In most sharks, the crushing power of the jaws is secondary to the damage done by the sharpness of the teeth. Once the shark grasps its prey, it immediately shakes its head from side to side. The razor-sharp teeth melt through flesh like butter and cut through bone like a chainsaw.

The mouth on most sharks is well behind its long nose. Looking at the animal, it's difficult to imagine how a shark manages to bite anything at all. Wouldn't that nose get in the way? People used to believe that sharks roll over on their sides to attack. But it turns out evolution has nicely solved this problem too. When a shark bites, it dislocates its jaw, thrusting it forward and (in many species) even past the end of its long nose! If the action can be slowed so the human eye can catch it, you're in for an awesome sight. (I first saw it when running one of my shark films in slow motion.) In many species, like the blue shark, most of the teeth are well concealed behind the shark's gums. When the blue shark attacks its prey, the jaw shoots down and out to the end of its nose, revealing a tangle of sharp teeth. Once grasped, the jaw pulls the prey back and in. It all happens in the blink of an eye.

You might think that evolution would have arranged a simpler solution to the problem of the shark's long nose by, say, putting the mouth at the front end and skipping the nose altogether.

But the shark's nose is also very useful. Riddled with pores called the Ampullae of Lorenzini, these tiny sense organs provide critical information to help sharks find their prey.

The senses available to the shark as it hunts are as elaborate as the sensory apparatus of a jet fighter. When a jet pilot searches for a target, he first uses radar. As he closes on the target, he locates the enemy aircraft visually. Finally, the missile he fires may use heat to guide it to the target. A shark uses a similar system. As it closes on its target, different sensory mechanisms come into play.

Sharks can hear low-frequency sounds produced by a struggling or injured fish more than half a mile away. They use internal ears, and their hearing is integrated with another sensory organ called the lateral line which detects minor pressure changes in the water. Using both mechanisms, the shark detects and pinpoints the position of an underwater sound source. The sounds produced by struggling fishes occur in very low frequencies, many too low for human hearing. The shark's acoustic senses are tuned specifically to these frequencies.

As it rushes toward the sound of the injured fish, the shark may begin to detect blood in the water. The shark's sense of smell is incredibly acute. It begins smelling fish blood in concentrations as low as one part in ten million! And as the shark swims, it determines the direction of increasing concentrations of blood. Even if the fish stops struggling, the shark has it firmly targeted.

How well a shark sees depends on the amount of light and the clarity of the water. Whatever the conditions, the shark's excellent visual acuity will maximize them. Many shark species have extremely light-sensitive eyes. Some species can see in almost total darkness. As the shark closes on its target, it begins to see its prey as soon as water clarity permits. Using vision, the shark rushes up to the prey and opens its mouth. As the jaw dislocates and lunges forward, the shark covers each eye with an eyelid called the nictitating membrane. This membrane protects the eye from any injury the prey might inflict. In the final moments of the attack the shark cannot see, but it is far from blind.

This is where that long awkward nose comes in. The small pores called Ampullae of Lorenzini are arranged in lines that rim and criss-cross the shark's nose. The Ampullae detect the tiny electrical field produced by the circulation of

blood within the fish and the contraction of its muscles. Using the Ampullae of Lorenzini, the shark makes its final attack.

Sharks can sense incredibly weak electrical fields. If you hooked up a single flashlight battery and connected it to two electrodes 1,000 miles apart, its electrical field would be within the shark's astounding sensory range. Scientists speculate

SHARK HABITATS

Which sharks hide and hunt on the sandy bottom? Wobbegongs, for instance. Skate-like angel sharks. And this large nurse shark.

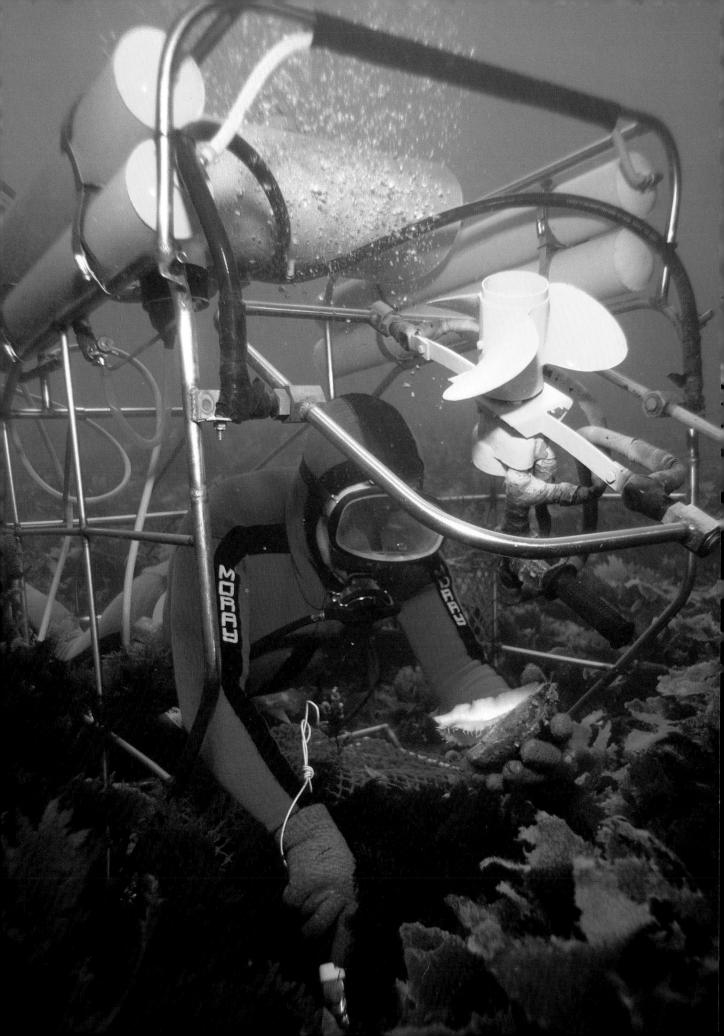

hat this ability to detect weak electrical fields may be so acute that sharks can sense the earth's own magnetic field. They may use magnetic lines of force for navigation to migrate great distances through open ocean.

The sensitivity of sharks to electrical fields may also explain why sharks get so disoriented around metallic objects such as shark cages, metal boat hulls, or propellers. The huge electrical fields produced by these objects must be as disorienting to a shark as a trumpet blown right into your ear!

Folk wisdom has it that sharks feed on anything from people to old shoes to discarded license plates. Although some unusual things have been found in shark stomachs, equally strange things have been found in the stomachs of humans. I once read about a boy who swallowed a wristwatch. I also read about a man whose hobby was eating his Rolls Royce luxury car (he expected it would take about ten years to finish the meal). But just as most people are selective about the things they eat, sharks usually limit what they eat to shark foods. Which foods do sharks prefer? Well, for most species it's fish.

Sharks make their living eating various kinds of marine life. Different species have different diets. Mako sharks eat fast-swimming tuna and mackerel. Blue sharks eat slower-swimming fish and squid. Horn sharks eat crabs and mollusks. Great white sharks eat seals and sea lions.

The two largest species of sharks eat an almost-microscopic diet. As they swim majestically through the sea, basking sharks and whale sharks strain the water they swim through to feed on tiny plankton animals. Both these giant sharks have very small teeth which they don't really use in the feeding process.

Most species of bony fishes release tremendous numbers of tiny eggs into the ocean. The hatchlings are usually quite small. Only a tiny fraction of a percentage ever survive to reach maturity. Sharks,

IN AUSTRALIA, ABALONE DIVERS MUST WORK IN A CAGE. WHY? BECAUSE MANY SHARKS IN THESE SHALLOW WATERS ARE BIG AND FAVOR BIG PREY. IN COMMON WITH OTHER SHARKS, THIS GREAT WHITE CAN SENSE BLOOD IN THE WATER FROM A DISTANCE. UNIQUE AMONG SHARKS, THE GREAT WHITE ALSO SEES WELL OUT OF WATER, OFTEN CIRCLING BOATS AND STARING AT YOU WITH A COLD BLACK EYE.

ALTHOUGH THIS GREAT WHITE *shark has been deliberately attracted to the cage with the diver in it by using fish as bait, it's quite easy to see what might happen to an unprotected diver at this point.*

on the other hand, have evolved more sophisticated reproduction strategies. Why? Like other predators at the top of the food chain, sharks exist in much smaller numbers than their prey. Sharks produce only a small number of offspring. But baby sharks enter the world well developed and quite capable of survival. A much greater percentage of them survive to become adults than the countless tiny offspring of bony fishes.

All sharks reproduce through one of three mechanisms: viviparity, ovoviviparity, or oviparity. Viviparity is very similar to human reproduction. Viviparous sharks develop inside the mother's womb over a period of many months. The unborn sharks derive nutrition from their mother through a placenta very similar to the kind found in mammals. At the completion of their development, a small number of well-developed baby sharks are born live and ready to take their place in the ecosystem. This is the kind of reproduction found in mako sharks, white sharks, blue sharks and other types of requiem sharks.

Ovoviviparous reproduction is rather unusual. The mother shark produces well-developed eggs, but she doesn't lay them. Instead, the babies hatch inside the mother's womb. After the baby sharks use up the food supply provided in their yolk sacs, they satisfy their hunger by eating their brothers and sisters. Talk about sibling rivalry!

By the time the mother is ready to give birth, only one shark remains in the womb. This last baby has already proven itself to be the strongest, most aggressive, and best prepared to survive in the wild. Ovoviviparity is the way sand tiger sharks reproduce.

Oviparous sharks lay eggs. Unlike the tens of thousands of tiny eggs laid by bony fish, ovi–parous sharks lay a small number of large, well-protected eggs. Horn sharks and swell sharks reproduce in this manner. Their leathery eggs blend

THE WHALE SHARK, A GENTLE GIANT UP TO 40 FEET OR MORE, TOLERATES ANY NUMBER OF HITCHHIKERS, FROM A HUMAN DIVER TO AN ASSORTMENT OF REMORAS OR SUCKER FISH ATTACHED AROUND ITS MOUTH. WHALE SHARKS LIVE ON TINY PLANKTONIC ANIMALS, WHICH THEY TAKE IN BY FILTERING THROUGH THEIR GILL SLITS.

in with the seaweeds that cover the bottom where the sharks live. The eggs contain a very large yolk sac, where the baby shark grows before hatching, some ten months later.

The largest shark in the sea, the whale shark is also the largest fish. Besides being over 50 feet long, it can tip the scales (if it had any) at over 20 tons. That's 40,000 pounds! This oviparous hulk lays the largest eggs in the world. How do we know? One – and only one – has ever been seen. It was caught in a net in the Gulf of Mexico in 1953. The egg was a foot in length and contained a baby whale shark 14 inches long. I've often wondered about that egg and tried to imagine that very private place somewhere on the ocean floor where these 50-foot-long leviathans go to lay their eggs. That I would like to see!

In 1973, Peter Benchley wrote the novel *Jaws*. The book achieved great success, sold millions of copies and inspired a motion picture that made more money than any other film had ever made. The popularity of the novel and film underscored just how much people fear sharks.

People tend to fear what they don't understand. Most humans have never seen a wild shark and know almost nothing about them. They know so little about the true nature of sharks that most could not tell whether the characteristics of the great white shark in the film were imagined or real. After all, it's true that sharks do sometimes bite people and occasionally these attacks are fatal.

Of course, many things kill people which would prove relatively uninteresting as best-selling novels or hit motion pictures. Hundreds of thousands are killed in automobile accidents. An equal number are killed by inhaling cigarette smoke. But people continue to drive cars because it's convenient and to smoke cigarettes for no good reason at all. Ironically, most of those who continue to smoke despite the knowledge that cigarettes may cause a painful and often fatal disease, would be terrified at the thought of swimming in waters where a 10-foot shark had been seen. They would probably continue to be afraid even if I told them that sharks almost never bite human beings. Almost never.

Those of us who dive and have seen dozens, hundreds, or even thousands of wild sharks know just how infrequent "almost never" is. Most golfers don't fear lightning when they go out on the golf course since people are almost never struck by lightning. Each year, about 550 people are struck by lightning in the U.S. The average number of Americans attacked by sharks each year is less than 12. Now that's "almost never." Experi–enced divers know this, and diving with sharks is something we look forward to and enjoy.

Perhaps much of the primal human fear of sharks comes from imagining the degree of our helplessness and the shark's supposed viciousness. The idea of swimming in deep water, unable to see into the depths that conceal a rising shark, unable to swim away at any speed significant to a shark, totally vulnerable and unable to defend yourself as the animal dismembers you... this is a terrifying vision. Very occasionally this sort of thing happens, but it is extremely unusual.

It's common to read or hear that sharks are savage, mindless feeders that will eat almost anything. In movies, you've often see sharks portrayed as enjoying the taste of humans as much as they relish fish. But all those millions of years of evolution has produced a creature with superior sensory capabilities. Sharks know what they eat. They are no more likely to eat a human than you are to eat a wristwatch. Certainly, sharks do bite people and occasionally a boy will swallow his father's wristwatch. But both occurrences are quite unusual.

Most shark attacks occur when a shark mistakes a swimmer for something it normally eats. These

LIKE OTHER SHARK SPECIES, THE GREAT WHITE HAS DARK COLORING ABOVE AND WHITE BELOW, ENABLING IT TO 'DISAPPEAR' AGAINST ITS BACKGROUND. SOME SHARKS HUNT EACH OTHER, SO CAMOUFLAGE SERVES TO PROTECT. BUT MOST USE IT TO STALK FISHES, TURTLES, MOLLUSKS, SEA LIONS, WHALES, AND OTHER PREY.

HUMANS HAVE ALWAYS BEEN VERY CURIOUS ABOUT SHARKS. STUDY IN THE WILD IS DIFFICULT, SO SCIENTISTS USUALLY TAG SHARKS IN SOME WAY. FOR THOSE WHO WORK WITH SHARKS, PROTECTIVE STEEL MESH SUITS HAVE BEEN PERFECTED. AS THESE TRIALS SHOW, SHARKS OFTEN HAVE TO BE ENCOURAGED WITH PIECES OF FISH BEFORE THEY WILL BITE HUMANS.

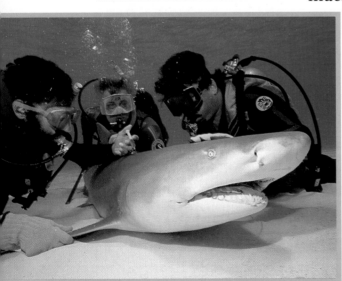

attacks happen most frequently in murky water. As soon as a shark bites a human, it generally realizes it has made a culinary error. Often the attacks are more like "tastes" than "bites." If a one-ton shark really wanted you for breakfast, you'd have little or no chance of survival. Yet even attacks by the most feared of all sharks, the great white, are survived by two-thirds of the victims. Divers can sometimes provoke attacks without meaning to. The blood and noise produced by speared fishes can bring sharks close in for confrontations. Underwater photographers often use baits to attract sharks within camera range. (Some of the photos in this book could not have been achieved otherwise.) Other divers are so unafraid of sharks that they will try to grab one by its tail, which can have embarrassing and painful consequences. More often than not, however, divers are disappointed in their efforts to approach sharks underwater. One year I spent four weeks diving in the South Pacific and never got close enough for one good photo. Sharks generally fear divers much more than divers fear sharks. And for good reason.

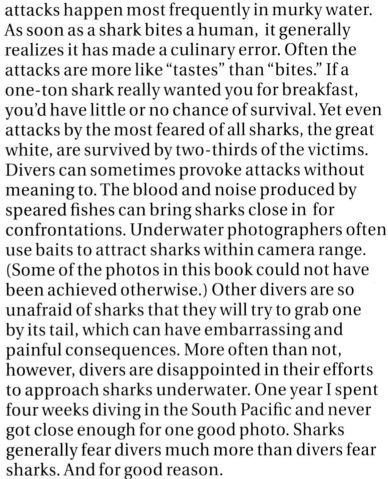

Sharks have been called the ultimate killing machines. But there's another large predator on this planet that makes the shark's voraciousness pale to insignificance. This creature has wiped out hundreds of animal and plant species and continues to push more into extinction each day, including entire populations of sharks. This creature is the most terrible creature-eater of all: man.

Humans kill hundreds of millions of sharks each year. Half of them, we eat. Many we kill in the process of catching other fish. And a shameful number we kill just for fun. We now know that sharks are long-lived creatures that reproduce slowly. Their populations cannot take the impact of unregulated and indiscriminate fishing. And so their numbers are decreasing in most oceans of the world. Lemon and thresher sharks are probably the most threatened species.

NOT ALL SHARKS MATCH OUR IDEAS OF THEM. TAKE THE WOBBEGONG, A SHARK OF THE SOUTH PACIFIC THAT LOOKS MORE LIKE A SPOTTED BLOB WITH FRINGES. MANY WOBBEGONGS PREFER SHALLOW WATER; A FEW EVEN LEAVE THE SEA BRIEFLY TO CLIMB FROM ROCK TO ROCK. SLEEK HUNTERS OR SHAPELESS BOTTOM DWELLERS, EACH SHARK SPECIES HAS ITS OWN FASCINATION.

But who cares if we kill off all the sharks? Who will miss them? Perhaps the same people who now miss rhinos, tigers, elephants, and other species that dangle over the precipice of extinction. These animals have also killed humans from time to time. But these wonderful creatures are what makes wilderness wild! Without them, our lives are less exciting and the richness of life on earth is diminished for everyone.

Who will miss the sharks? I will! Hundreds of thousands of sport divers will! Most importantly, our children and theirs will miss the sharks. More and more, the generations to follow ours will look to the oceans for the wilderness experiences soon to become rare on land.

MORE ABOUT SHARKS

ABOUT THE AUTHOR & PHOTOGRAPHER

During his 20-plus years of filming and photographing, Howard Hall has been nose-to-nose with sharks of many species. Educated as a marine zoologist, Howard began as a cameraman and later as director or producer for dozens of films about sharks. He now concen–trates on producing marine wildlife documentaries seen by audiences throughout the world. His list of credits and awards includes five Emmys. A contributing editor for *International Wildlife* and *Ocean Realm*, Howard has also written several books, including *The Kelp Forest* and *A Charm of Dolphins*.

RECOMMENDED BOOKS & FILMS

• *Sharks of North American Waters*, by Jose Castro (Texas A & M, 1983).
• *National Geographic* 1982 documentary on sharks, widely available at public libraries, with Howard Hall as cameraman.

SPECIAL THANKS

Janet Posen, Science Resource Teacher for San Diego City Schools.

WHERE TO SEE SHARKS IN THE WILD

Diving trips specifically to see sharks are available from a number of tour companies to a variety of locales, including: Southern California, Southern Australia, off Florida, Hawaii, and the Bahamas; and in Mexico's Sea of Cortez.

WHERE TO SEE SHARKS IN CAPTIVITY

Many aquaria and marine parks around the world exhibit sharks. A growing number of them show the animals in their habitats, from coral reefs to sandy bottoms. The list below is just a starting place.

U.S.A.:
Pacific Coast: Seattle Aquarium; Pt. Defiance Aquarium; Marine World/Africa USA; Steinhart Aquarium; Monterey Bay Aquarium; Sea World of San Diego; Scripps Aquarium.

Atlantic Coast: New England Aquarium, Boston; Mystic Marinelife Aquarium; New York Aquarium; New Jersey State Aquarium; Virginia Marine Science Museum; National Aquarium of Baltimore; 3 Aquaria in North Carolina; Sea World of Florida; Marineland of Florida; Miami Seaquarium; Theater of the Sea in Islamorada; EPCOT Center.

Elsewhere: Gulfarium, Florida; Aquarium of the Americas, New Orleans; Sea-Arama Marineworld, Galveston, Texas; Sea World of Texas; Dallas Aquarium; Sea World of Ohio; New Indianapolis Zoo; Shedd Aquarium, Chicago; Aquarium of Niagara Falls; Pittsburgh Aqua Zoo; Fleishmann Aquarium at Cincinnati Zoo; Waikiki Aquarium and Sea Life Park, Hawaii.

CANADA:
Vancouver Public Aquarium; Montreal Aquarium

BIG GULP

This 20-ton giant is called 'the whale shark' for good reason. It's twice the size of a large killer whale! Like a baleen whale, the whale shark feeds on tiny sea-going animal and plant morsels called plankton. Swimming with its mouth open, the whale shark takes in water and strains it through its gills.

How does the whale shark find its some-times-microscopic food? Easy. It just keeps moving. Think of the sea as soup, the plankton and a few squid and sardines as the 'noodles,' and the whale shark as a huge and gentle diner.

FAST FACTS GLOSSARY & INDEX

SHARK BODY PARTS

• **CARTILAGE** (pages 5,8) – A tough, elastic animal tissue. Sharks, rays, and chimaeras have cartilage instead of bone.

• **FINS** (pages 2, 9)

    • **Pectoral fins** (pages 2, 9) – Located on the chest; the slower the cruising speed, the larger the fins.

    • **Finning** – Decline of the shark population is due in part to 'finning,' the practice of cutting off the animal's fins and throwing the body back into the ocean to die. Dried fins are used in Asian folk medicines. More than seven million pounds a year go into shark-fin soup, which sells for $50 a bowl in Asian restaurants.

• **SKIN** (page 12) – Sandpaperlike surface reduces drag in water.

    • **Denticles** (page 12) – Small, sharp toothlike structures that cover the skin. Like teeth, they wear off and are replaced by larger denticles.

• **TAIL** (pages 9, 10)

    • **Heterocercal tail** (page 9) – Large lobes on the top of tail keep a shark's nose up and its tail down to avoid sinking.

    • **Homocercal tail** (page 10) – Top and bottom lobes nearly the same size. Makos and others that cruise at high speed don't need larger lobes to push up the nose.

• **TEETH** (pages 12-13) – Hundreds of teeth, arranged in up to eight rows, grow out of a shark's skin, not its skeleton. When worn, they're replaced by new, larger ones. In some species that can be about 30,000 teeth in a lifetime.

GIVING BIRTH

• **OVIPARITY** (page 33) – (ovo = egg + parity = birth) – a small number of egg sacs are laid by the mother; young develop inside.

• **OVOVIVIPARITY** (page 33) – (ovo = egg + vivi = living + parity = birth) – the mother produces eggs whose young hatch in her womb. After depleting the food supplies in the yolk sacs, the young eat each other. Only the strongest one is born.

• **VIVIPARITY** (page 33) – (vivi = living + parity = birth) – Like human reproduction with young developing in the mother's womb; born live.

SENSES

• **HEARING** (page 24) – Can hear low-frequency sounds of a struggling or injured fish more than one-half mile away. Internal ears work with lateral line to pinpoint location of sound.

• **SIGHT** (page 25) – Extremely sensitive to light; some species can see in almost total darkness.

    • **Nictitating membrane** (page 25) – This third eyelid found in some species protects the shark's eyes from being injured while attacking prey.

    • **Tapetum** (page 8) – Iridescent membrane in the eye lets sharks see well in near-darkness.

• **SMELL** (page 24) – Incredibly acute; sharks often called 'swimming noses.' With nostrils wide apart, a shark can tell which side its prey is on and zero in on target.

• **OTHER SENSES**

    • **Ampullae of Lorenzini** (pages 24, 25) – Tiny sense organs that crisscross a shark nose and detect minute electrical fields in a prey's blood and muscle contractions.

    • **Lateral line** (page 24) – Located along the sides of the head and body. Detects minor pressure changes in the water; works with hearing to find source of sound.

HOW SHARKS HELP HUMANS

• CARTILAGE – An extract from shark cartilage is used to make artificial skin for burn victims. Researchers think a cartilage protein that stops blood-vessel growth may help curb tumors, some glaucoma, and arthritis in humans.

• EYES – Shark lenses are used in some human cornea transplants. Sharks don't develop cataracts.

• IMMUNE SYSTEM – Shark blood has antibodies that resist bacteria, viruses, and chemicals toxic to humans. Shark wounds heal quickly, and their bodies may hold keys to help human injuries do the same.

• LIVER – Shark liver oil with vitamin A is the main ingredient in hemorrhoid medicine.

• SKIN – Because of its rough texture, sharkskin was once used as sandpaper to polish wood. Cured skin without the denticles is used as durable leather for shoes and other products.

CLOSE-UP
A Focus on Nature

Here's what teachers, parents, kids, and nature lovers of all ages say about this series:

• • • • • • • •

"High-interest topics, written in grownup language yet clear enough for kids..."

"Dazzling, detailed photos. Your beautiful books have a strong educational component—keep it up!"

"Packed with facts and priced right for busy adults."

"Extremely useful for students with reading difficulties..."

"Your book is the best souvenir we could have of our whale-watching trip."

"These books are great gift items for all the bird-watchers, divers, and wildlife artists on my list!"

Silver Burdett Press books are widely available at bookstores and gift outlets at museums, zoos, and aquaria throughout the U.S. and abroad. Educators and individuals wishing to order may also do so by writing directly to:

SILVER BURDETT PRESS
299 JEFFERSON ROAD,
PARSIPPANY, NJ 07054

◆ HABITATS ◆

The Desert
Hot & dry but it's home to big cats, coyotes, & more

The KELP FOREST
The ebb and flow of life in the sea's richest habitat

Life at the Frozen Edge
ICEBERG AND GLACIERS

Tropical RAINFOREST

Coral Reefs

Tidepools
THE PACIFIC WORLD OF THE ROCKY SHORELINE

◆ ANIMALS ◆ BIG & SMALL

BEARS

Insects
All about ants, aphids, bees, fleas, termites, toebiters, & a beetle or two

A CHORUS OF FROGS

ELEPHANTS

165 million years of DINOSAURS

Butterflies
Monarchs, moths & more — up close & unexpected

◆ BIRDS ◆ IN THE WILD

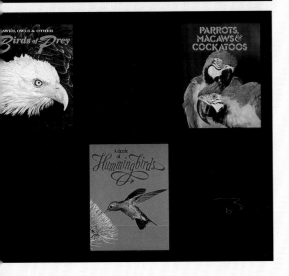

HAWKS, OWLS & OTHER Birds of Prey

PARROTS, MACAWS & COCKATOOS

A dazzle of Hummingbirds

◆ MARINE LIFE ◆

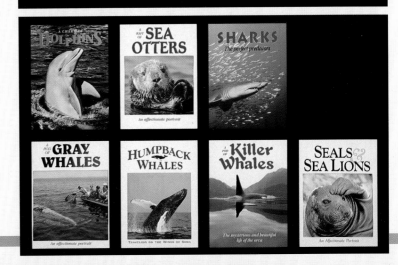

A CHORUS OF DOLPHINS

A RAFT OF SEA OTTERS
An affectionate portrait

SHARKS
The perfect predators

A POD OF GRAY WHALES
An affectionate portrait

HUMPBACK WHALES
TRAVELING ON THE WINGS OF SONG

A POD OF Killer Whales
The mysterious and beautiful life of the orca

SEALS & SEA LIONS
An Affectionate Portrait

*"Sharks and other predators
at the top of the food chain
don't get much human
sympathy. Yet they need
our protection as much
or more than other species.
If sharks no longer roamed
our seas, the mystery and
majesty of the ocean itself
would be diminished."*

– Howard Hall